MIA HAMM

SOCCER LEGEND

T0016353

BY CHRÖS McDOUGALL

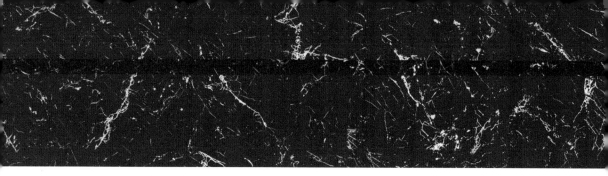

Book design by Jake Nordby
Cover design by Jake Nordby

Photographs ©: Kevork Djansezian/AP Images, cover, 1; Andy Lyons/Allsport/Getty Images Sport/Getty Images, 4; Scott Audette/AP Images, 6; Rick Stewart/Allsport/Getty Images Sport/ Getty Images, 8; David Madison/Getty Images Sport/Getty Images, 11, 18, 25; Barry Thumma/ AP Images, 13; John T. Greilick/AP Images, 14, 30; David Cannon/Allsport/David Cannon Collection/Getty Images, 16; Paul Hawthorne/Getty Images Entertainment/Getty Images, 20–21; Lutz Bongarts/Bongarts/Getty Images, 22; Jamie Squire/Getty Images Sport/Getty Images, 26; Red Line Editorial, 29

Press Box Books, an imprint of Press Room Editions.

ISBN
978-1-63494-788-6 (library bound)
978-1-63494-808-1 (paperback)
978-1-63494-847-0 (epub)
978-1-63494-828-9 (hosted ebook)

Library of Congress Control Number: 2023909019

Distributed by North Star Editions, Inc.
2297 Waters Drive
Mendota Heights, MN 55120
www.northstareditions.com

Printed in the United States of America
012024

About the Author

Chrös McDougall is an author, editor, and sportswriter who regularly covers soccer as well as Olympic and Paralympic sports.

TABLE OF CONTENTS

1 CAN'T STOP HER

The clock ticked past 45 minutes when Michelle Akers booted the ball to Mia Hamm. The star US forward headed the ball to midfielder Kristine Lilly. Then Hamm burst up the field.

The United States was facing Brazil in a friendly match on May 22, 1999. Nothing was on the line. Yet more than 10,000 cheering fans looked on at the Citrus Bowl in Orlando, Florida. They were there to witness history. Hamm was ready to make it happen.

Mia Hamm carries the ball forward in a game against Brazil in 1999.

The US team surrounds Hamm (9) after she scored her 108th international goal.

With one touch, Lilly sent a looping pass to Cindy Parlow at the top of the penalty area. A soft volley placed the ball right in the path of Hamm as she charged toward the goal.

Hamm's hard touch sent the ball deep into the penalty area. She sped to the ball before a defender could get to it. Then she drilled a right-footed shot through the legs of Brazil's goalie.

At 27 years old, Hamm was already playing in her 172nd game for the United States. She was the face of the national team. Fans were drawn to the star player. She was both fierce and humble. And now Hamm had 108 international goals. That passed Italy's Elisabetta Vignotto for the most of all time—male or female.

The 1990s was a time of explosive growth for women's sports in the United States. Perhaps no sportswoman was as popular as Hamm. And her historic summer of 1999 was only getting started.

2 ON THE RISE

Mariel Margaret Hamm, known as Mia, was born on March 17, 1972, in Selma, Alabama. The year Hamm was born, the United States passed a new law known as Title IX. It required schools to offer girls and boys equal opportunities. This led to a massive growth in popularity in girls' sports. Hamm was part of the first generation of girls who grew up with Title IX.

Mia's dad was in the US Air Force. This meant the family had to move a lot.

Mia Hamm poses for a picture while playing for the US women's national team.

They lived briefly in California. Soon after, they moved to Florence, Italy.

It was in Italy where Mia began loving soccer. Even as a toddler, her talent was clear. Mia joined her first team at age five while living in Texas. By high school, her skills set her apart from other girls her age.

Women's soccer was still a young sport at the time. For years, officials had discouraged or even barred women from the game. But those attitudes were changing during the 1980s. And in 1985, the US women's national team was founded. One year later, coach Anson Dorrance discovered Mia. But Dorrance was skeptical. Mia was only 14. The coach agreed to watch Mia play, but he didn't want anyone to tell him which player she was. It took only a few seconds for him to figure it out.

Anson Dorrance addresses the University of North Carolina women's soccer team in 1994.

The following year, in 1987, Mia played in her first game with the national team. That made her the youngest player in team history. Two years later, she joined the soccer team at the University of North Carolina. Dorrance coached that team, too. The Tar Heels were a force in college soccer. Hamm thrived with them. She was a relentless worker who always wanted to improve. In her four seasons, the Tar Heels won four national titles. Hamm led the nation in goals three times.

Hamm wrapped up her college career in 1993. That's because she'd taken the 1991 season off to focus on the national team. That year, the first Women's World Cup was held in China. At 19, Hamm was the youngest player on the US team.

THE FAB FIVE

Mia Hamm played her first game with the national team in a friendly on August 3, 1987. Fellow teens Joy Biefeld (later Fawcett) and Kristine Lilly also debuted in the 2–0 win over China. Brandi Chastain and Julie Foudy joined the team in 1988. Together they became known as the "Fab Five." The group went on to play together until 2004.

The US women's national team visits President George H. W. Bush after winning the 1991 Women's World Cup.

The aggressive US squad featured a trio of star forwards in Michelle Akers, April Heinrichs, and Carin Jennings. For this reason, Hamm played mostly as a midfielder. She appeared in all six games, starting five of them, and scored two goals. After beating Norway 2–1 in the final, Hamm and the US team were the sport's first women's world champions.

3 AMERICAN STAR

By the 1995 Women's World Cup in Sweden, Mia Hamm had taken over as the star forward for the United States. This time she started all six US games and scored two goals. However, the Americans ended the tournament in third place.

More opportunities for Hamm and her teammates were coming. The 1996 Olympics were held in Atlanta. For the first time, the event featured a women's soccer tournament. Fans came out in huge

Hamm's 147 assists are the most in US soccer history.

Hamm dribbles by two Chinese players in the 1996 Olympic gold-medal game.

numbers to watch. Hamm didn't disappoint

them. In the first game of the tournament, she

scored a goal and added an assist to lead the

United States to a 3-0 win against Denmark. The United States went on to face China in the final, held in Athens, Georgia. In the 68th minute, Hamm began an attack up the right side of the field. Then she passed to Joy Fawcett, who fed the ball to Tiffeny Milbrett for the go-ahead goal to make it 2-1. In front of 76,481 fans—the most ever at a women's sporting event—the Americans held on to win the gold medal.

An ankle injury had slowed Hamm during the Olympics. After the final, the injury prevented her from joining her teammates in a victory lap. Nonetheless, her popularity was soaring. And so was the popularity of women's soccer. Hamm and her teammates had become inspirations to the girls watching at home, such as future US star Alex Morgan. Female soccer

Hamm signs autographs for fans after a friendly against Argentina in 1998.

players now had a template to build on in Hamm.

On the field, no player was as dangerous. Hamm's elite speed and fearlessness helped her pile up goals. She was also a skilled playmaker and a fierce competitor. In 1998, she had her best season with 20 goals and 20 assists in 21 games. Then, on May 22, 1999, she became the all-time leading scorer in international soccer.

Off the field, Hamm was modest and even shy. In 1999, a major magazine asked Hamm to pose for its cover. Hamm declined, saying she didn't want the focus to be only on her. Her

THE MIA HAMM FOUNDATION

One of Mia Hamm's brothers, Garrett Hamm, died of a rare blood disorder in 1997. Two years later, she created the Mia Hamm Foundation. It raises money to support others with the same disorder, called aplastic anemia. The foundation also supports opportunities for girls in sports.

humility made her even more popular. With the Women's World Cup coming up that summer on home soil, she had become one of the most famous athletes in the United States.

ALL EYES ON MIA

As her popularity grew in the late 1990s, Mia Hamm was everywhere in the media. She was a guest on a popular late-night TV show in 1996. *People* magazine featured her in a special issue in 1997. Nike named a building at its headquarters after Hamm. She was featured on the iconic Wheaties cereal box. And she even had a video game named after her.

However, she was perhaps best known for a 1997 Gatorade commercial. It featured Hamm and basketball superstar Michael Jordan. They went head-to-head in a variety of sports as the song "Anything You Can Do (I Can Do Better)" played. Sharing the screen with Jordan helped people see a top female athlete on the same level as a top male athlete.

Mia Hamm (middle) stands next to Senator Hillary Clinton (second from right) at the 2005 premiere of *Dare to Dream*, a documentary about the 1996 Olympic US women's national team.

4 SOCCER ICON

The US national team opened the 1999 Women's World Cup with a match at Giants Stadium in New Jersey. Hamm took center stage right away. She controlled a bouncing pass as she ran down the right flank. With a quick move, she tapped the ball back, dodging a Danish defender. Then Hamm smashed a left-footed strike into the top of the net. A sellout crowd of 78,972 fans roared.

The tournament proved to be a landmark event in women's sports. The

Hamm prepares to take a corner kick during the 1999 World Cup.

opener was a sign of what was to come. As the United States kept winning, crowds kept coming out—many of them wearing Hamm's No. 9 jersey. Hamm scored again in the second game. Then she drew a key penalty in the semifinals. A record crowd of 90,185 packed the Rose Bowl in California for the final. After a 0-0 draw, the United States defeated China in a shootout. All five US players, including Hamm, scored in the shootout. The game captivated US audiences like no women's sporting event had before.

The next step for women's players was creating a professional league. In 2001, Hamm helped start the Women's United Soccer Association (WUSA). Two years later, she helped the Washington Freedom win the 2003 WUSA championship. However, the league

Hamm waves to the crowd as the United States celebrates its 1999 Women's World Cup victory.

struggled to take off and folded right before the 2003 World Cup. The tournament had been moved to the United States on short notice, so there was less time to plan and sell tickets.

Hamm (second from left) celebrates with her teammates after winning the 2004 Olympic gold medal.

Hamm scored twice and recorded five assists, but the US team finished third.

The 2004 Olympics were in Athens, Greece. Hamm and longtime teammates Julie Foudy and Joy Fawcett announced it would be their last tournament. They were determined to go out on top. Hamm scored in the first two games. The Americans got to the final against Brazil. In extra time, teammate Abby Wambach scored to secure the gold medal.

Hamm officially retired after a farewell game in December. In 276 international games, she scored 158 goals. Wambach and others would go on to break that record as women's soccer continued to grow. That all happened, though, because Hamm and her teammates showed what was possible.

SOCCER LIFER

Since retiring, Mia Hamm has stayed close to the game. In 2014, she was announced as one of 22 owners of Los Angeles Football Club. The men's pro team debuted in Major League Soccer in 2018. She also has roles with men's teams AS Roma and FC Barcelona.

TIMELINE

1. Selma, Alabama (March 17, 1972)
Mariel Margaret "Mia" Hamm is born.

2. Tianjin, China (August 3, 1987)
At age 15, Mia Hamm becomes the youngest player ever to play on the US women's national team.

3. Chapel Hill, North Carolina (November 22, 1993)
Hamm wraps up her college soccer career at the University of North Carolina with her fourth national title.

4. Athens, Georgia (August 1, 1996)
Hamm and the US women defeat China 2-1 to win the first Olympic gold medal in women's soccer.

5. Orlando, Florida (May 22, 1999)
Hamm scores her 108th international goal to become the all-time leading goal scorer in international soccer history.

6. Pasadena, California (July 10, 1999)
In front of a record crowd of 90,185, Hamm and the United States win their second Women's World Cup after defeating China.

7. Washington, DC (April 14, 2001)
Hamm and the Washington Freedom win the first WUSA game 1-0 over the Bay Area CyberRays at RFK Stadium.

8. Athens, Greece (August 26, 2004)
In Hamm's last major tournament, the United States beats Brazil 1-0 in extra time to win the Olympic gold medal.

MAP

N

29

Birth date: March 17, 1972

Birthplace: Selma, Alabama

Position: Forward

Size: 5-foot-5 (165 cm)

Teams: North Carolina Tar Heels (1989–93), US women's national team (1987–2004)

Women's World Cups: 1991–champion, 1995–third place, 1999–champion, 2003–third place

Olympic Games: 1996–gold, 2000–silver, 2004–gold

Major awards: FIFA Women's World Player of the Year (2001–02), Women's Sports Foundation Sportswoman of the Year (1997, 1999), US Soccer Women's Player of the Year (1994–98), MAC Hermann Trophy (1992–93)

GLOSSARY

aggressive
Likely to attack.

assist
A pass that results in a goal.

debuted
Made a first appearance.

extra time
Two 15-minute periods added to the end of a soccer game that is tied after regulation.

friendly
A soccer game that's not part of an official competition.

generation
A group of people who are all born around the same time.

modest
Not being overly proud of one's own abilities.

shootout
A way of deciding the winner of a soccer game that is tied after extra time. The teams take turns shooting penalty kicks.

skeptical
Having doubts.

volley
A shot by a player while the ball is in the air.

TO LEARN MORE

Books

Lowe, Alexander. *G.O.A.T. Soccer Strikers*. Minneapolis: Lerner Publications, 2022.

Mattern, Joanne. *Trailblazing Women in Soccer*. Chicago: Norwood House Press, 2023.

Shaw, Gina. *What Is the Women's World Cup?* New York: Penguin Workshop, 2023.

More Information

To learn more about Mia Hamm, go to **pressboxbooks.com/AllAccess**.

These links are routinely monitored and updated to provide the most current information available.

INDEX